Contents

Published and printed by Maxiprint, Kettlestring Lane, Clifton Moor, York YO3 4XF

© *Tony Rablen 1996*

ISBN: 1 871125 27 8

The Tidewater Way

The *Tidewater Way* is a long-distance footpath right across northern England from tidal water to tidal water, from Lancaster on the River Lune to Ulleskelf on the River Wharfe – 90 miles of peaceful and scenic footpaths through the Yorkshire and Lancashire Dales. The Way is ideal for anything from a leisurely ramble across the country, to a 24 hour 'coast-to-coast' challenge.

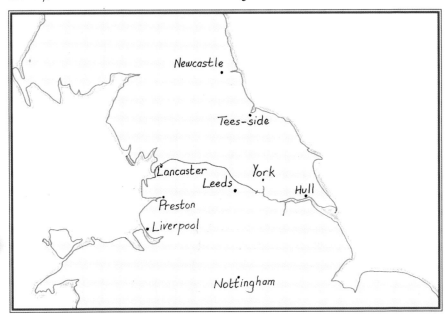

About the Way

The route lays vigorous claim to being a coast-to-coast walk: it goes from Normal Tidal Limit to Normal Tidal Limit – and on O.S. maps the N.T.L. is the point on an estuary where the river colour changes to sea colour, and the line marking the coast begins.

But, unlike A. Wainwright's classic coast-to-coast route, the *Tidewater Way* takes a short and easy line across the country. From West to East, the route lies beside the River Lune, and then up a tributary valley, that of the River Wenning. The Pennines are crossed near Malham Tarn, and then the route lies along Wharfedale, often on the riverbank, sometimes along the valley side. So the Way is typically along easy field footpaths and through farms and small villages in the valleys, with shorter stretches across the hills. Along Ilkley Moor and over Malham Moor are the only sections where the Way briefly crosses unenclosed land.

The route has a pleasing symmetry, as befits a cross-the-country walk. The western and eastern ends are in the broad, mature valleys of the Lune and the Wharfe; then come sections of gritstone valleys and upland; and the central section is the limestone hills of the Pennines.

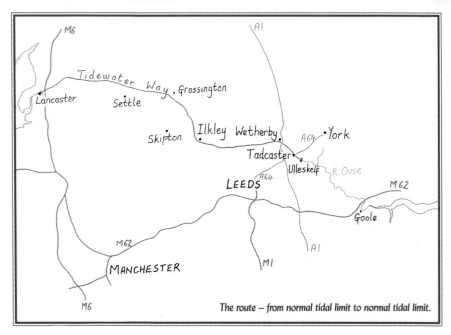

The route – from normal tidal limit to normal tidal limit.

Finding the two ends of the Way is not difficult. Remarkably both Lancaster and Ulleskelf have their own railway stations. Otherwise, the Lancaster end is only a mile from junction 34 on the M6, whilst Ulleskelf is on the B1223, a few miles south-east of Tadcaster.

I first formulated the idea of a short coast-to-coast walk in 1990. As a resident and native of Yorkshire, I decided to see if I could devise a route across Yorkshire and Lancashire which a fit person could complete in 24 hours. The shortest crossing proved to be from the N.T.L. on the River Ribble at Preston across to Ulleskelf, and I completed the crossing in 1991. But the route was not brilliant: there was a lot of rough ground, some sections were scenically mediocre, and the route-finding was often difficult. So, for a few extra miles, it seemed worth trying a Lune-Wharfe route and this turned out to be an excellent route, scoring highly on all the criteria that I set for a walk. Unfortunately the extra miles made the route too long for me to complete in 24 hours – I failed dismally in 1992. But two years later, by taking to roads through the night, I completed the crossing in 23 hours 50 minutes.

For your interest, the criteria which have governed my choice of route for the *Tidewater Way* are as follows:

1. **Legality**: the whole route is to be on public rights of way or permitted paths.
2. **Directness**: the route is intended to be as direct as possible, maintaining a good line over both short and longer distances.
3. **Integrity**: the route is intended to be a quiet footpath. Therefore, public roads are to be avoided, and tarmac in general, except in villages.
4. **Cleanliness**: the route is 'clean' to the extent that it is:
   – scenic – easy-going under foot – easy to navigate and negotiate.

Using the Way

The most pleasant approach to using the Way is as a relaxed ramble, giving yourself time to enjoy its tranquillity and variety. Because almost all of the Way is easy-going underfoot, there is no requirement (in summer at least) for heavy walking boots, and as Malham Moor is the only section of any length which is remote and exposed, it is normally quite safe to travel fairly light.

But you will need overnight accommodation. Details of B & B accommodation are available from the National Park Authority on 01756 752774, or the Yorkshire and Humberside Tourist Board on 01904 707961. B & B accommodation is most scarce at the western end of the Way. The following are useful: Hornby – Castle Hotel (015242 21204), Royal Oak (015242 21228), Mrs. Shuttleworth (015242 21053). Low Bentham – The Punch Bowl (015242 61344), The Stonegate (015242 61362), Mrs. Frankland (015242 61813). At Stainforth there is a Youth Hostel (01729 823577) or the Craven Heiffer (01729 822599), but from here to Threshfield/Linton – the highest section of the Way – there is nothing. The only way to break this long day is to make a descent via Malham Cove to Malham for a night.

For those who want to walk the Way in shorter sections (perhaps one day at a time), the simplest way is to go with someone else and use two cars. However, there are, in fact, reasonable bus services covering the route of the Way – and the western end is served also by the railway - but getting accurate information is not always easy. The National Park Authority (01756 752774) publishes annually a compendium of summer bus and rail timetables called 'Dales Connections', and this is the best place to start.

Some, however, will want to use the route as a 24 hour challenge. The key issue here is the choice of which section to traverse in the night. I have two recommendations. If you are fit enough to manage the route as it stands, then the section along Wharfedale from Linton to Ilkley is navigationally the easiest. An easier alternative, however, is to use roads by night; this is quicker and can often be a few miles shorter.

Those completing the Way in under 24 hours are invited to enter their details in the *Tidewater Way Record Book*, held at the The Ship Inn, Ulleskelf (01937 832202). And all users of the Way are invited to write in (with any sponsorship money – cheques made payable to Christian Aid) to the following address: *Tidewater Way, c/o 171 Burton Stone Lane, York YO3 6DG.* Your details will then be entered on our Register, and you will be sent a Certificate of Completion.

The route was originally designed for walking; but since some users will want to run the route, some alternatives have been added for their benefit. Stiles are a nuisance to the runner because they break the rhythm – so some pleasant alternatives to stile-infested sections are included.

Other alternatives are included because of a conflict of route selection criteria – for example, the alternative route through Bramhope (see page 26) is more direct, but involves more roads. At the western end of the route is the longest alternative offered – the North bank alternative (see page 9-11). This alternative is slightly longer and uses more roads than the main route but the riverbank section is more varied and less exposed. Another alternative in this category is the Newby Moor alternative (see page 13). This alternative reduces somewhat the length of road-walking, but the moor itself is rough, tussocky ground. Locating the 'prominent sheep-trod' is the key to a successful crossing, but it is not easy: a leisurely reconnaissance trip is recommended. Certainly, if you are under a time constraint, you are strongly advised not to attempt the Newby Moor alternative without prior reconnaissance. To do so is to risk losing time, temper and energy – and, probably, dry socks!

However you are using the Way – hopping, skipping, running or plain walking, please always adhere to the Country Code:

- Fasten all gates. Do not climb over gates, except as a last resort.
- Keep to the right of way; do not trespass.
- Use stiles; never climb over walls or fences.
- Keep dogs under control at all times.
- No fires.
- Take your litter away.
- Respect all crops and wildlife.
- Leave livestock and machinery alone.

About the maps

The maps are designed with only one purpose in mind: navigating the *Tidewater Way*. Therefore only information relevant to that purpose is included. This makes them very easy to use.

Across the centre of each map page is a map strip at scale 2½" to 1 mile. Above the map are any directions for eastbound walkers; below the map are any directions for westbound walkers.

Things essential to navigation – for example, walls, stiles, rivers, barns etc. – are accurate at the time of going to press. Small scale detail is not always accurate – for example, the exact arrangement of buildings in a farmyard – but enough detail is given for navigational purposes. The amount of detail shown varies with the difficulty of the navigation. So, for example, where the Way follows a road, little other information is given, but where the Way crosses open fields, every wall and barn is shown.

Consistent with our semi-metricated state, the maps show heights in metres, and distances in miles and yards!

For a fuller appreciation of the countryside along the Way, you are recommended to buy the appropriate O.S. maps, which are:

Landranger maps: 1:50,000
97 Kendal & Morecambe
98 Wensleydale & Upper Wharfedale
104 Leeds & Bradford
105 York

Or, for greater detail:

Pathfinder maps: 1:25,000
648 Lancaster & Morecambe
637 Burton-in-Kendal & Caton
650 High Bentham & Clapham
Outdoor Leisure 10 - Yorkshire Dales (South)
671 Keighley & Ilkley
672 Harewood
673 Tadcaster

Using the maps

These maps are designed for ease of use. But if you are inexperienced at map-reading, I offer you two golden rules:

1. Always follow the map and not a path on the ground. Remember that the red **Tidewater Way** line on the map does not mean a visible path, except where it is marked as on a road or track. At all other times it is wisest to assume that the Way is not visible on the ground. If you follow a path on the ground, you are likely to end up at a sheep trough! So, always follow the map.

2. Always have multiple reference points, not just one. So, never say to yourself: "This next bit is easy: I just follow the river until I come to a gate." But rather say: "The river should bend to the right, then I should pass a farm on the left, and when the field narrows, I should come to the next farm gate." Then, if perchance the farmer has removed the gate and six feet of walling to make an easy access for his new muck-spreader, you won't be caught out – or hopefully not!

   And finally....
   GOOD LUCK – and enjoy yourself.

Bolton Abbey

Speaking personally

I am enormously grateful to God for the privileges of health, freedom and prosperity which have enabled me for many years to gain great pleasure from walking in the Dales; and so, when the possibility of writing up this walk arose, it seemed only right and proper to use the proceeds from the sale of this book to support Christian Aid, who minister to those many whose lives are marked by the complete absence of these – and many other – privileges. If you feel at all similarly, you will find a photocopiable sponsorship form at the back of this book. Money should be returned to (cheques made payable to Christian Aid): Tidewater Way, c/o 171 Burton Stone Lane, York YO3 6DG.

Relaxing at Skerton Weir after the 24-hour crossing

But alongside this idealism is the reality that this book would not have been born without the help of several people: John Eckersley, a good friend, whose enthusiasm and vision have sustained me; Mark Comer, a member of my church youth group many years ago, who has provided the photographs and overseen all the page layout and the printing; Richard Pearson, a next-door neighbour, for his delightful illustrations; and Charles Hart for designing the cover.

My thanks to you all, and to many others who have helped in lesser ways.

Tony Rablen.

Key to maps

S	Stile - ladder-stile, step-stile, or squeeze-stile.	? ?	Trees, deciduous and evergreen.
G	Small gate - kissing-gate, bridleway-gate or pedestrian-gate.		Slope, where relevant
FG	Farm gate.	▼▼▼▼	Rocky edge - beware!
↦	Finger-post, pointing along Way. Location and direction of symbol not accurate.	·217	Spot height, approximate, in metres
		▲2.74	Exact height at hill-top or trig. column.
╲	T.W. on footpath. It should not be assumed that this represents anything visible on the ground.	▪▪	Buildings: accurate as to location, but not to shape or size.
╲	T.W. on unsurfaced vehicular track, enclosed and unenclosed.		Field boundary - wall, hedge or fence - intact and broken.
╲	T.W. on unsurfaced tractor track; T.W. leaves track.	⊥ ⊥ ⊥	Rough, tussocky ground; boggy when in blue.
╲	T.W. on tarmac road, enclosed and unenclosed.		
╌╌	Alternative T.W. route.		Railway line, in use and disused.
╲	Directional note: above the map for Eastbound walkers and below the map for Westbound walkers.		River, with direction of flow, and weir.
⬜	Instruction for walkers in either direction.	NTL	Normal Tidal Limit
			National Grid lines, in 1 kilometre squares, showing North.
⋅	Arrow identifying Way-side feature.		
(6·84)	Miles to Lancaster and Ulleskelf.		

8

LANCASTER

The massive Skerton Weir is the Western end of the Tidewater Way; it is the absolute tidal limit on the River Lune - all tides reach it and none goes beyond it.

Access to the weir is on foot only - beside the HSS Hire Shop and Swan Bearing Factors building on the A683 is a short footpath which gives access to the old railway line.

HALTON (Upper Weir)

Apart from a minor diversion to reach Skerton Weir itself, the whole of this section is along the old Lancaster-Wennington line. It is now converted into a cycle/footpath, and known as the Caton Trail. The way-marked Lune Valley Ramble also follows the old line, which makes an excellent and easy way in and out of Lancaster.

The 18th century canal aqueduct and the 20th century motorway bridge make an interesting contrast of style and material. Those wishing to avoid the tarmac section of the line may use the rougher riverside path along much of its length.

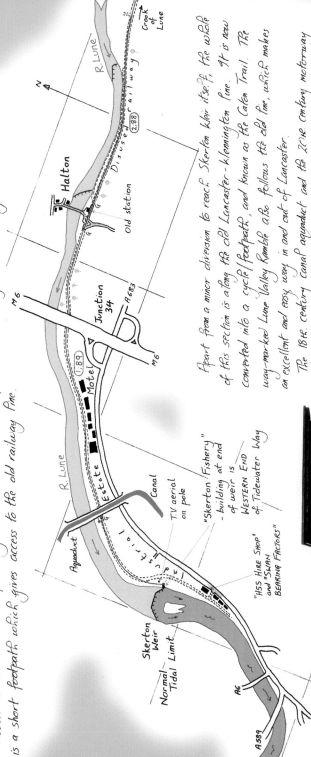

Skerton Fishery building

Navigation ★   Terrain ★

© Crown copyright

HALTON (Upper Weir)

The River Lune here flows gently and majestically in a wide, deep channel. At the western end, the valley is narrower, and the incised meander at Crook of Lune is both pretty and impressive – a favourite place for picnics and swimming. Upstream, the valley is broad, and the river meanders across an expansive flood-plain.

AUGHTON BARNS

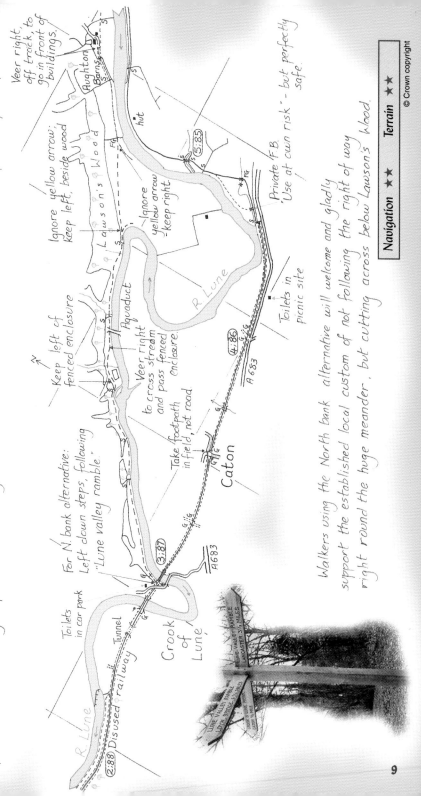

Veer right, off track, to go in front of buildings.

Ignore yellow arrow; keep left, beside wood

Ignore yellow arrow – keep right

Aughton Barns

hut

Lawson's Wood

R. Lune

⑤:85

Private FB. "Use at own risk – but perfectly safe.

Toilets in picnic site

④:86

A 683

Keep left of fenced enclosure

Veer right to cross stream and pass fenced enclosure.

Aqueduct

N

Take footpath in field, not road

For N. bank alternative: Left down steps, following "Lune valley ramble"

Caton

③:87

A 683

Toilets in car park

Crook of Lune

Tunnel

Disused railway

R. Lune

②:88

Walkers using the North bank alternative will welcome and gladly support the established local custom of not following the right of way right round the huge meander, but cutting across below Lawson's Wood.

Navigation ★ ★ ★	Terrain ★ ★

9

R. HINDBURN

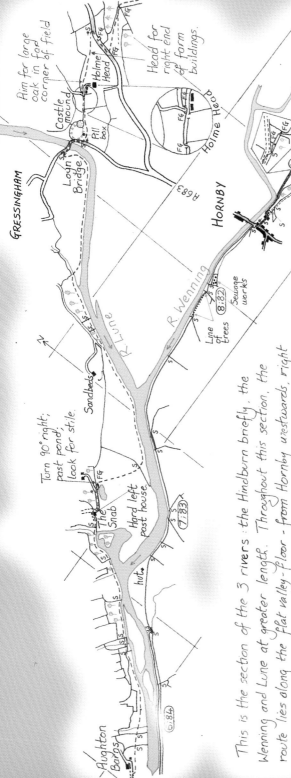

Map labels:

Aim for large oak in far corner of field

Head for right end of farm buildings.

Holme Head

Ignore sign on gate.

Stile at end of hedge.

GRESSINGHAM

Castle mound

Pill box

Loyn Bridge

A 683

HORNBY

Aim for Hornby Castle

9.81

Stile at end of wire fence.

Sewage works

R. Hindburn

R. Wenning

R. Lune

Old rly

Line of trees

8.82

Sewage works

N

Sandbeds

Turn 90° right; past pond; look for stile.

The Snab

Hard left post house.

hut

7.83

6.84

Aughton Barns

This is the section of the 3 rivers: the Hindburn briefly, the Wenning and Lune at greater length. Throughout this section, the route lies along the flat valley-floor - from Hornby westwards, right along the riverbank. The flood-plain of the Lune is here very broad, and it gives a wild, expansive, featureless feel to this part of the Lune: relieved by the river itself and its rich bird life.

On the North bank, the flood-plain is narrower and backed by hills. This makes the North bank alternative more varied and less exposed. Hornby Castle - part ancient, mostly more recent - is a prominent and attractive landmark in the valley.

Navigation ★ ★ ★	Terrain ★ ★

R. HINDBURN

ESKEW HILL

A truly rural section. The Way here is very little walked and navigation is a constant challenge. Greenfold Gill is rough: walkers in shorts, go carefully!

- Over stile.
- Scramble down and left to stream.
- Cross stream.
- Up and diagonally right.
- Find stile by big oak.

Aim for half-buried rock in field; look for flimsy stile.

- pass front of house;
- left round side;
- right through gate.

- Cross flimsy stile into wood.
- Head diagonally right, then straight down.
- Cross stream.
- Up and slightly left to find stile.

Go to solitary tree in field; down middle of field; look for gap stile.

Stile at base of oak tree.

Aim for left of house.

Head left of ash tree; look for small stile.

Head for left end of barn.

Aim for trees on hill-top.

- Aim for solitary tree.
- At tree, 30° left.
- At hedge, left to find stile in short section of wall.

Cross stile by barn, turn right; look for gap stile in short length of wall.

Aim for solitary tree in field; Look for gap stile

Aim for FG on road

Go through r. hand of 3 FGs.

Stile by tree.

Aim for house.

For Mealbank

Through gate-stile on corner; walk round storage tower.

Keep to wall on right

Keep walls on left in view; aim left of large oak

Gate to left of leaning oak

Head well right of barn

Ignore sign on gate.

Keep uphill; follow line of old hedge

① No stile; climb fence.
② Stile overgrown.

Stile at end of hedge

Aim for Hornby Castle

Stile at end of wire fence.

Barn Windy Bank 126

Shed

House

Park House

Tatham

Old railway

R. Wenning

R. Hindburn

See previous page

Old rlwy.

Works

Wray

Greenfold Gill

Eskew Hill

Robert Hall

Perries Fm.

Greenfold Gill

School Hill

Barn

(12.78)

(11.79)

(10.80)

(9.81)

N

11

GREYSTONEGILL LANE

12 **ESKEW HILL**

E→W Head slightly downhill, for gate by 2 trees

Take Fg on right, just past 1:9 sign

Barn

Linghaw

House — Shed — Fg

Fg

Batty Farm

- Up between buildings into yard;
- diagonally right across yard;
- right through gate.

Head left of farm.

Linghaw Farm

16.74

R. Wenning

Keep right through gate.

Ridding Lane

Through farmyard; over metal step-stile

Staggarth

- Through gate into yard
- Diagonally left across yard to for corner
- Down lane between buildings

- Over metal step-stile into farmyard
- At end of buildings, go through gate on right.

15.75

N

High Bentham

Caravan Site

R. Wenning

Moulterbeck Farm

Cross stream; fork right for stile into caravan site.

14.76

- Follow line of uprooted hedge and between old gate-posts; aim for right end of farm buildings

Low Bentham

Stile in hedge may be overgrown

Cloudsbank

Leave river-bank; keep uphill

Cross stream up steep bank.

- From the gate, take a bearing on the left end of small, corrugated-iron feed-bin just ahead.
- Maintain this course, over brow of hill and down across Large field.
- Look for stile into wood.

Eskew Beck

Eskew Hill

13.77

Aim for solitary tree on skyline on hill; left at hedge.

This is a very pastoral stretch of the route — a succession of farms, fields and riverbank, but no villages and refreshingly little tarmac. In both directions the navigational task is easiest in the riverside section; away from the river, vigilance is required.

Eskew Beck is the Lancashire/N. Yorkshire boundary; appropriate ceremonies may be performed on the foot bridge!

Navigation ★★★ **Terrain** ★★

© Crown copyright

CRINA BOTTOM

GREYSTONEGILL LANE

Those wishing to reduce the length of road-walking on this section may choose to take the "Newby Moor alternative," but please see the warning on p.5 before deciding.

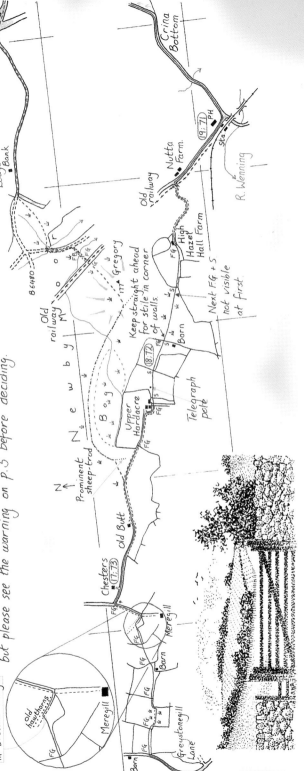

2 old gate-posts in broken hedge

Old hawthorns

Meregill

Greystonegill Lane

Barn

Meregill

Barn

Chesters
[17.73]

Old Butt

Prominent sheep-trod

N

N e w b y   M o o r

B o g

Upper Hardacre

Telegraph pole

Old railway

Gregory 177

Keep straight ahead for stile in corner of walls

Next F.G + S not visible at first

Barn

[18.T7]

High Hazel Hall Farm

Old railway

Nutta Farm.

Sta

R. Wenning

[19.71] PH

Crina Bottom

B6480

Lodge Bank

A65

In terms of terrain, Newby Moor, a typical gritstone upland area, is the hardest part of the whole route. The short section of unimproved moorland (⊔) is rough, tussocky, and sometimes wet; also, to a lesser extent, the western section between Meregill and Greystonegill Lane. The area is a favourite haunt of curlew and lapwing, and has a pleasant sense of wildness about it.

Navigation ★ ★ ★   Terrain ★ ★ ★

© Crown copyright

13

At Clapham, two boundaries are crossed: the National Park boundary and the gritstone / limestone boundary. In practical terms, this means that East of Clapham, the way-marking is better, and the ground smoother, drier and grassier.

The Feizor-Clapham section scores very highly on all the criteria (see p. 3) and is a great pleasure to walk.

The walled lane from Feizor to Wood House Farm is an alternative especially attractive to runners, who will be glad to avoid a further 11 stiles.

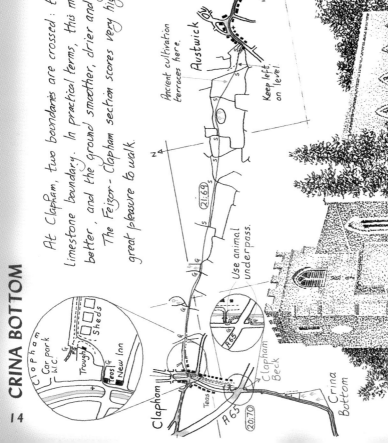

Clapham Church

Navigation ★ ★   Terrain ★ ★

Feizor

(23.67)

Wood House Farm

Barn

Austwick Beck

(22.68)

Ancient cultivation terraces here.

Austwick

Keep left, on level!

N

(21.69)

Use animal underpass.

Clapham Car park W.C.

Trough

Sheds

Teas

New Inn

Clapham

Teas

Clapham Beck

A65

Crina Bottom

(20.70)

WINSKILL STONES

FEIZOR

This is a very pleasant, airy section through typical limestone country.

The going underfoot is generally excellent, but the uneven steps through Stainforth Scar are dangerously slippery if wet.

The section involves 400m of ascent and descent.

Stainforth Bridge is delightful - and is well seen from a recommended detour to the Force.

Stainforth

FP STAINFORTH 1¼

Next ladder stile is hidden in dip; keep straight on.

Upper Winskill

Lower Winskill

26:64

Stainforth Scar

Cattle grid

1:350

Winskill Stones

Left over stile by double gates, for "Stainforth Langcliffe."

Stainforth

Carlisle

Settle

B6479

R. Ribble

190

Little Stainforth

25:65

Caravan Site.

Force

FG

Follow direction of footpath sign, keeping right, to track visible at top of slope.

320

Smearsett Scar ▲363

24:66

Pot Scar

Feizor

210

Stainforth Force

Navigation ★★★   Terrain ★★

15

LANGSCAR

This is the 'summit section': 462m. at Langscar Hill is the highest point of the walk, and the East-West watershed. Malham Moor is rather bleak - in the central part the limestone is covered by peat which makes the ground rough and wet - but the views to the West and North are ample reward.

The tractor track across the moor gets sketchy in places, but is always discernible with care.

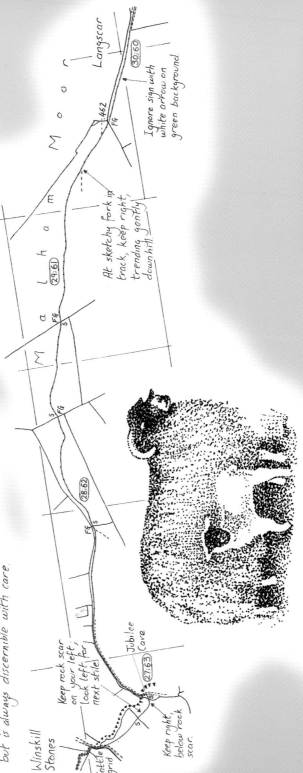

M a l h a m   M o o r

Langscar

N↗

29:61

28:62

27:63

30:60

·462

Ignore sign with white arrow on green background.

At sketchy fork in track, keep right, trending gently downhill.

Jubilee Cave

Keep rock scar on your left; look left for next stile!

Keep right, below rock scar.

Winskill Stones

Cattle grid

Scenically, this section is dominated by the impressive dry valley below the water-sinks and leading on down to Malham Cove – a good place to pause awhile.

Mastiles Lane is an old drove road, linking different sheep farms owned by the monks of Fountains Abbey; they once owned much land in this area.

The O.S. boldly mark the Roman Camp on Mastiles Lane, but locating it on the ground is quite another matter – but it is fun trying.

At Gordale Beck, the older, impervious rocks which underlie Malham Tarn are briefly exposed; geological faulting has brought them to the surface in this area.

Navigation ★ ★   Terrain ★ ★ ★

Kealcup

Mastiles Lane

FG

FG

(33:51)

Roman Camp

Gordale Beck

FG

FB

FG

Mastiles Lane

FG

(32:58)

Wall and stile not visible; estimate direction and then go 5° further left to reach wall S.E. of stile; turn right at wall for stile.

Malham Tarn

N

↑ Pennine Way

Water-sinks

S

SL

Pennine Way

(31:59)

G

Watlowes

– Join path coming up from Watlowes.

– Turn left over ladder stile.
– Up by wall on right, for Langscar Gate.

– Over ladder stile and turn right.
– Go 30 yds, then fork left for Watersinks.

Langscar

Cattle grid

S

FG

Keep to wall.

SKIRETHORNS

This is a very varied section, ranging from the rough upland around Mastiles Lane, through Limestone pastures, a steep side-valley, and Wharfedale valley-floor. Over 330 metres of ascent and descent is involved.

There is an amazing concentration of walls West of Height Lathe - was this the H.Q. of a nineteenth century Community Programme ??

At FG on left, turn right through gap in broken wall, aim for plantation.

Aim for FG in lane wall

Kealcup

·373

·390

34·56

Bordley

Bordley

FG

FG

·320

S

35·55

·384

Fork left off track at 2 stone troughs, to descend hill by wall on left.

Aim for barn

Lime-kiln

Barn

N↗

Height Lathe

Height Ho. S

FG

S

S

36·54

S

S

Through caravan site, on past "Reception."

Wood Nook Caravan site

S

Skirethorns

·200

37·53

- Follow drive past "Reception";
- through gap in wall;
- on up to top left corner of site.

Geological faulting means that for much of this section, there is limestone to the North and gritstone to the South. Between ·320 and Wood Nook, the contrast in landscape (and wall colour!) is particularly marked.

SKIRETHORNS

HEBDEN Suspension Bridge

This is a very pretty section of the route: the suspension bridge, Linton and Skirethorns are all very attractive, but the jewel in the crown is Linton church – a beautiful building in a charming, riverside setting.

The stepping stones at Linton are kept in good repair, and should present no problems in normal conditions; the alternative is offered just in case......

East of the stepping stones, the route follows the Dales Way and is well-walked.

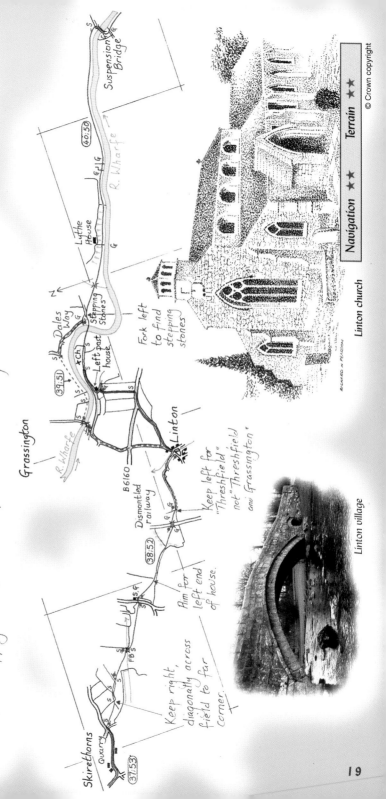

Suspension Bridge

40:50

R. Wharfe

Luthe House

Dales Way

Stepping Stones

39.51

Ch.

Left past house

Fork left to find stepping stones

Grassington

R. Wharfe

Linton

B6160

Dismantled Railway

38.52

Keep left for "Threshfield" not "Threshfield" and Grassington"

Aim for left end of house.

Keep right, diagonally across field to far corner.

Skirethorns

Quarry

37.53

Linton church

Linton village

Navigation ★ ★   Terrain ★ ★

RICHARD W PEARSON

19

HEBDEN Suspension Bridge

HOWGILL

This section provides some splendid river scenery - especially between Howgill and Woodhouse - where the river is alternately placid and wild. Between Burnsall and Howgill, the river crosses from limestone to gritstone - contrast the scenery at Haugh Wood with that around Loup Scar.

Burnsall is deservedly popular as a beauty spot. The village boasts a seventeenth century grammar school, and a rather grand church - as well as the Red Lion, so conveniently located for Tidewater Way walkers.

The whole of this section is along the route of the Dales Way.

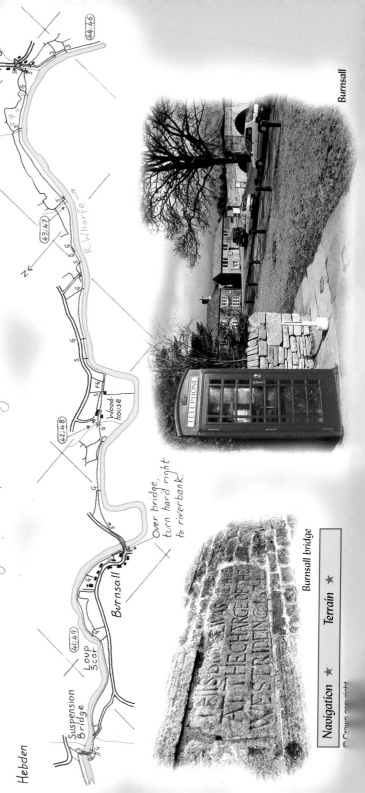

Burnsall

Burnsall bridge

| Navigation ★ | Terrain ★ |

© Crown copyright

HOWGILL

BOLTON ABBEY BRIDGE

This section is entirely along the river-bank. It is deservedly popular, as an easy walk, full of interest, through a beautiful part of Wharfedale, featuring Bolton Priory and ruins, the Strid, Barden Bridge and Barden Tower.

Between Bolton Priory and Barden Bridge, either bank of the river may be used; the mean and/or moneyless should use the E. bank between Cavendish Pavilion and the aqueduct to avoid the entry charge (the woods are private), but they will forfeit easy access to the Strid and the informative Nature Trails.

Barden Bridge marks the half-way point; but only Eastbound walkers may begin to relax - the Eastern half is easier than the Western.

Keep to higher path

(48.42)

Memorial

B6160

Bolton Priory

Keep right, right, uphill.

Cavendish Pavilion (teas)

(47.43)

Climb away from river.

(46.44)

At Strid, ascend bank, then right

The Strid

Aqueduct

Path ascends into wood

Barden Tower

(45.45)

Barden Bridge

B6160

♦ Barden Tower

R. Wharfe

(44.46)

Howgill

N

Memorial – Bolton Priory

BOLTON ABBEY BRIDGE

ADDINGHAM Low Mill

There are three distinct parts to this section: an easy riverside section from Bolton Abbey to Lob Wood, a climb over gritstone pastures up to Highfield Farm and down, and the village of Addingham with its lovely church.

The alternative route from Addingham to Lob Wood along the Dales Way is less strenuous and easier to navigate — and has some good river scenery — but directness, variety and excellent views favour the main route.

Just South of the A59 is the Southern boundary of the Yorkshire Dales National Park.

Navigation ★★ Terrain ★★

© Crown copyright

Low Mill (housing)
52,38

Addingham
Hall

R Wharfe
North St. Police
Church St.
Main St.
W.C.
Post Office
Sch.
Sugar Hill
51,39
Turn left out of lane into field

High Laithe
Through gap
Near left, uphill
Caravan Site

Golf cse.
Highfield Ho.
FG
Farfield Farm
B6160
Old rlwy
FG
50,40
Avoid difficult stile
Highfield Farm
Gorse
220
Look for gap-stile and trees by barn.

Ruined barn with trees
Aim by walls for stile
Lob Wood
Old rlwy
Path under viaduct
A59
49,41
15"

R Wharfe
Bolton Abbey
B6160
48,42

N

Bolton Abbey

At Highfield Farm, the North Yorkshire / West Yorkshire boundary is crossed.

ADDINGHAM Low Mill

From the riverside pastures to the moorland above the Cow + Calf is a height difference of 200 m. - and 2 different worlds connected by Ilkley. Ilkley was a Roman settlement, but grew rapidly as a Victorian resort.

There is a multiplicity of paths on this part of the Moor - so navigate by prominent landmarks (the pine plantation, the footbridge, the Tarn, the covered seating) and choose a path to suit.

Low Mill is a very attractive modern housing development - it's a shame the access road is so dismal!

Map labels:

- The Grove
- Wells Walk
- Linburn Mews
- Pool
- Covered Seating
- Cow + Calf
- Danger! Quarry edge
- 210
- Fork right; aim for middle of trees
- Fork left at brow of hill to avoid tarmac paths
- The Tarn
- 55:35
- I l k l e y M o o r
- Sta
- Ilkley
- A65
- Playground
- Start of Dales Way
- Old Bridge
- Sports Centre
- 54:36
- .75
- Hadfield Farm
- Pumping Sta
- The Hollins
- A65
- R Wharfe
- 53:37
- Old Rd
- Low Mill (housing)
- Playground
- steps
- Museum
- Old Bridge - Ilkley
- N
- C.P
- CG
- G

◀ Dales Way
Bowness 73 M

Navigation ★★★   Terrain ★★★

COW AND CALF ROCKS

MENSTON

This section contains suburban streets, grazing fields and open moor. The short stretch of road at Burley Woodhead divides the moor from the fields. Ilkley Moor is steeped in history - the Way follows a pre-historic trade route along the edge of the moor, passing near the Pancake Stone with its pre-historic "cup markings." The Moor is classic gritstone upland - rough and wet - but offering panoramic views Northwards.

The series of fields and the lane between Burley Woodhead and Menston are full of small-scale variety and charm; and the Way takes a pleasingly direct line.

The famous Cow and Calf rocks lie below our route - but a detour below the cliffs can easily be made. The Calf rock has hand and foot holds cut in it for those who wish to brave an ascent.

- Diagonally across lane to track-side path;
- past footbridge;
- bear right, to pass station building on left;
- across car park;
- left along Newfield Drive.

Menston

Sta.

(59.31)

snicket

.150

Bleach Mill

(58.32)

Spring Bank Farm

Hag Farm

N

Burley Woodhead

Barks Crag

(57.33)

M O O R

Y

E

L

K

L

300

I

Pancake Stone

Use hotel as reference point for start of descent.

Hotel

(56.31)

Cow + Calf

DANGER! Quarry edge

Navigation ★ ★   Terrain ★ ★ ★

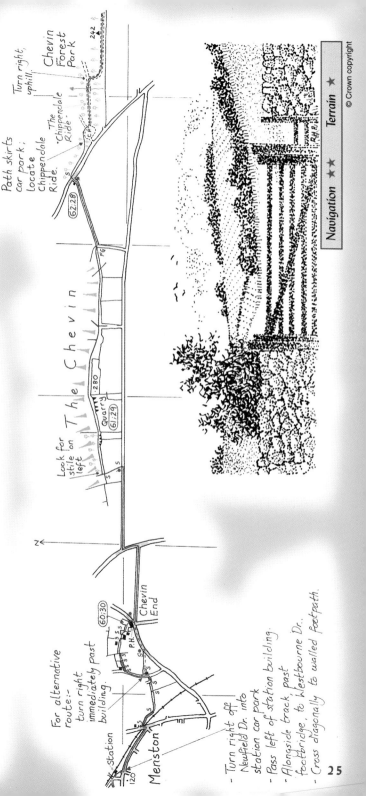

MENSTON

CHEVIN FOREST PARK

Otley Chevin is the Eastward extension of Ilkley Moor, and the airy walk along its Northern edge gives excellent views across Otley and lower Wharfedale. The prominent crag to the North is Almscliff Crag. The openness of the Chevin contrasts with the Forest Park - here the Chippendale Ride is a charming avenue of trees.

At Chevin End, the Leeds/Bradford boundary is crossed: Leeds to the East, Bradford to the West. Here the ground drops away steeply, with Menston lying over 158 metres below the Chevin.

Path skirts car park; locate Chippendale Ride.

Turn right, uphill.

The 'Chippendale Ride'.

Chevin Forest Park

242

C.P.

62.28

F.B.

Look for stile on left

The Chevin

280

Quarry

61.29

N

60.30

Chevin End

P.H.

For alternative route:- turn right immediately past building.

Station

Menston

120

- Turn right off Newfield Dr. into station car park
- Pass left of station building.
- Alongside track, past footbridge, to Westbourne Dr.
- Cross diagonally to walled footpath.

Navigation ★★   Terrain ★

© Crown copyright

CHEVIN FOREST PARK

ARTHINGTON BANK

This is a section full of interest and variety. In the West, the Way lies through pine woodland – and past our only trig. point, at 242 metres. Then comes Bramhope, firstly the old town and then the modern, wealthy outskirts. There are moments here when you are fairly sure you are trespassing up someone's drive, but fear not! – it's all a right of way. Finally, in the East, the Way lies along the top of the impressive Arthington sandstone quarry

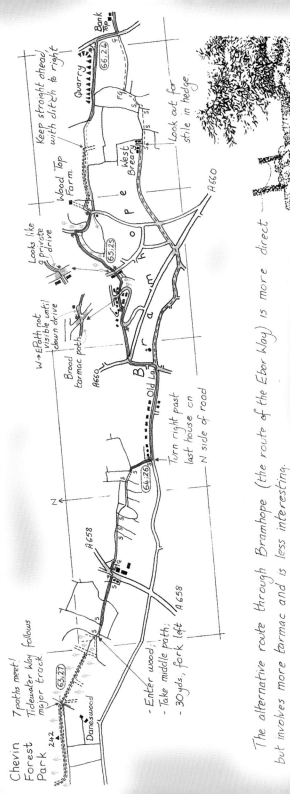

Chevin Forest Park

Chevin
Forest
Park
242 ▲

7 paths meet!
Tidewater Way follows
major track

- Enter wood;
- Take middle path;
- 30yds, fork left

Daneswood

A658

A658

63.27

N ←

64.26

Turn right past
last house on
N side of road

Old La

A660

B r a m h o p e

65.25

A660

W→E Path not
visible until
down drive

Broad
tarmac path

Looks like
a private
drive

Wood Top
Farm.

West
Breary

Keep straight ahead,
with ditch to right

Quarry

Bank
Top

66.24

Look out for
stile in hedge

The alternative route through Bramhope (the route of the Ebor Way) is more direct but involves more tarmac and is less interesting.

Navigation ★ ★ ★   Terrain ★

HAREWOOD BRIDGE

ARTHINGTON BANK

This is a very pleasant section through typical gritstone country, with fine views along lower Wharfedale. Although there is quite a stretch on roads, they are all quiet lanes, and enjoyable to walk. From Low Weardley to the A659, the route cuts through a corner of the attractive, wooded Harewood Estate.

There is about 170 metres of ascent and descent; but most of the descent goes to Eastbound walkers, as the Way descends steadily across Arthington Bank from Bank Top to Tinker Close, and then on down to the river at Harewood Bridge.

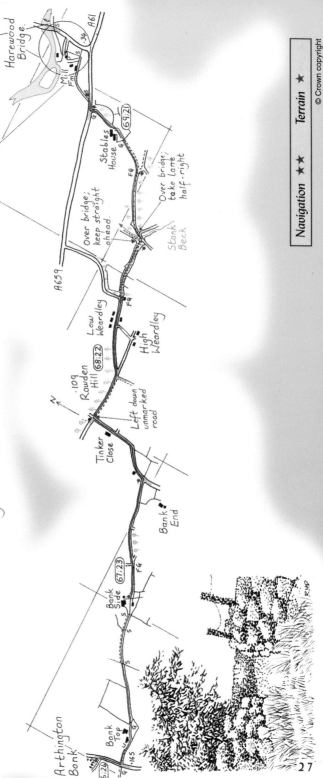

R. Wharfe →
Wood Mill
Office
Yard
Mill Fm.
A61
A659

Mill and Mill Fm.

Harewood Bridge.

A61

Mill Fm.

[69.21]

Stables House

Over bridge; take lane half-right

Stank Beck

Over bridge; keep straight ahead.

A659

Low Weardley

High Weardley

FG

•109
Rawden Hill

[68.22]

Left down unmarked road

N

Tinker Close

Bank End

[67.23]

Bank Side

FG

Arthington Bank

Bank Top

•165

[66.24]

RWP

HAREWOOD BRIDGE

CRABTREE LANE END

A61 Harewood Br.

Cross stream; shortly climb bank on right to gain field-edge.

Veer right and uphill to regain field edge.

R. Wharfe →

Netherby Deep

70:20

Tower

Approaching field corner:
- descend bank before beech tree
- cross stream
- left and up, to stile.

Veer right, off field edge, to pass through trees below tower.

71:19

N ←

72:18

Carthick Wood

R. Wharfe →

Climb over FG
Climb over FG

Road very dangerous - beware

73:17

A659

Crabtree Lane

Although the whole of this section lies within the Metropolitan County of W. Yorkshire — and the Northern outskirts of Leeds are only just over 3 miles South of Harewood Bridge — the Way here feels very rural — even remote. The river here, in contrast to the reaches upstream of Ilkley, flows in a deep, steep-sided channel; summer bathers have drowned in Netherby Deep.

In sharp contrast to the riverside tranquillity is the A659. This highly-regrettable, 600 yard dash along a narrow and busy main road is to be undertaken with great vigilance. Always walk in single file; always keep any children with you; try to face on-coming traffic.

Because of the danger, the landowner has kindly given permission for Tidewater Way walkers to use an alternative, riverside route. This is most welcome. But it is not a right of way and at present neither of the gates opens — they must be climbed over. Please be especially careful to protect crops and property along this concessionary alternative.

Navigation ★   Terrain ★

CRABTREE LANE END

WETHERBY

This section is the most Easterly in which it is possible to speak meaningfully of Wharfedale – as the ascents and descents between Crabtree Lane end and Woodhall bear out.

The road West of Linton, though tarmacked, is very quiet – it ends at Woodhall Hotel. The temptation to trespass along the hotel drive is very strong.... but should be resisted; the route via Sicklinghall House, though disastrously indirect, is quite pleasant. It is also a brief visit back to N. Yorkshire.

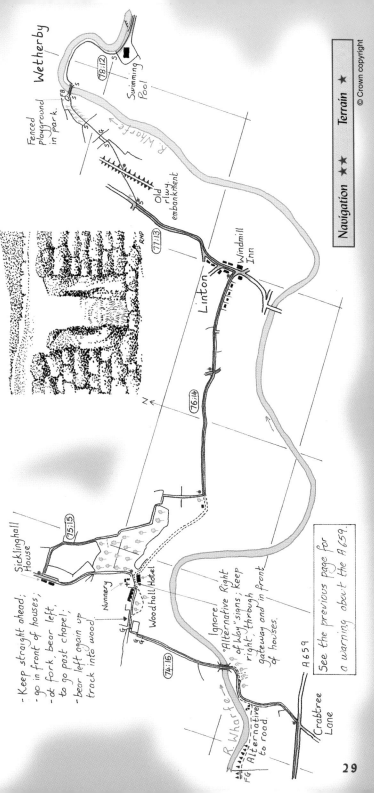

- Keep straight ahead:
- go in front of houses;
- at fork, bear left,
  to go post chapel;
- bear left again up
  track into wood

Sicklinghall House

Nunnery

Woodhall Hotel

75:15

74:16

Ignore "Alternative Right of Way" signs; keep right, through gateway and in front of houses.

A 659

R. Wharfe

Alternative to road.

FG

Crabtree Lane

76:14

N

Linton

77:13

RHP

Windmill Inn

Old r'lwy embankment

R. Wharfe

Fenced playground in park.

Wetherby

Swimming Pool

78:12

See the previous page for a warning about the A 659.

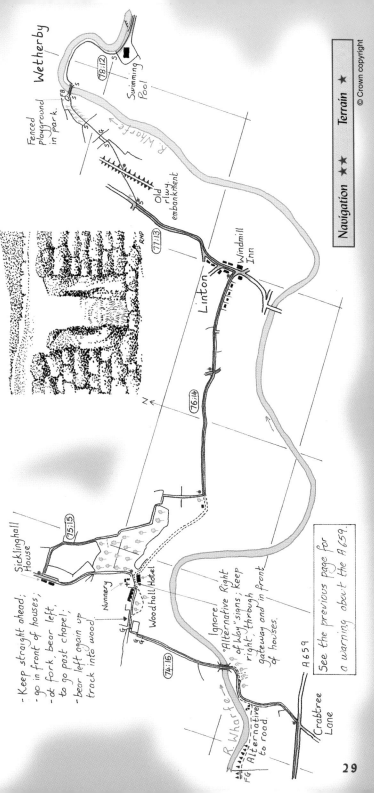

Navigation ★★   Terrain ★

WETHERBY   CARR BECK

The river here has cut a steep-sided valley into the magnesian limestone – and the route passes under low cliffs downstream of both Wetherby and Boston Spa. The tree-lined riverside walk in Boston speaks of the town's briefly-fashionable time as a spa.

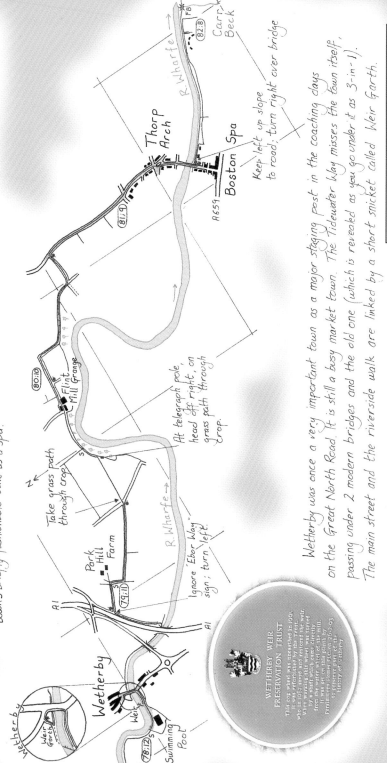

Wetherby

Weir Garth

Wetherby

Weir

Swimming Pool

78:12

Park Hill Farm

A1

79:11

Ignore "Ebor Way" sign; turn left.

R. Wharfe →

N

Take grass path through crop.

80:10

Flint Mill Grange

At telegraph pole, head off right, on grass path through crop.

6:18

Thorp Arch

A659

Boston Spa

R. Wharfe

82:8

Carr Beck

FB

Keep left up slope to road; turn right over bridge

WETHERBY WEIR
PRESERVATION TRUST

This cog wheel was unearthed in 19xx. It was refurbished by the Trust, who in 1982 [illegible] and restored the weir. When working this wheel was turned by a shaft which came directly from the water wheel at the mill. It was set in this [illegible] Preservation Stones PLC in 2002-03 to preserve part of the history of Wetherby.

Wetherby was once a very important town as a major staging post in the coaching days on the Great North Road. It is still a busy market town. The Tidewater Way misses the town itself, passing under 2 modern bridges and the old one (which is revealed as you go under it as 3-in-1). The main street and the riverside walk are linked by a short snicket called Weir Garth.

CARR BECK

TADCASTER

Tadcaster is an ancient crossing-place on the River Wharfe - used by the Brigantes before the Romans established a camp here - but now a town more famous for its breweries. The route through Tadcaster is very pleasant: past St. Marys church to the bridge and on and down a tree-lined avenue. The weir is the highest limit of tides on the Wharfe.

At Ingle Bank Wood the W. Yorkshire (Leeds District)/N. Yorkshire boundary is crossed.

Newton Kyme is a little gem with its graceful hall and pretty church looking out over open parkland and the impressive avenue of trees.

The river here is broad and deep, meandering slowly through the rich pasture-land.

Keep right along top of wall to F.B. and gate.

A659

Tadcaster

Weir

Old railway

R. Wharfe →

86.4

85.5

FG S

G

Newton Hall Kyme

84.6

FG

A659

83.7

S

Works

Ingle Bank Wood

W. Yorks. → N. Yorks.

old railway

Care needed: narrow path on bank edge

R. Wharfe

Carr Beck

FB

82.8

N

Newton Kyme Hall and Church

Navigation ★   Terrain ★★

31

Ulleskelf certainly doesn't feel very coastal - in fact, Spurn Point is nearly 60 miles away! But a few straggly cosier reeds in the bank suggest tidal water; and the Ship Inn tells of the days when Ulleskelf was a mooring place for ships riding the tide to Tadcaster. Many tides in fact reach Tadcaster, but the Normal Tidal Limit is Ulleskelf.

This really is the Flat-lands: not a hill in sight all along this section. Ulleskelf is a brick village, but at Tadcaster, the magnesian limestone was quarried and used for building.

The Ship Inn - the East end of the Way

 NTL

Ulleskelf

B1223

B1223

R.Wharfe

Line of old trees

Duck under barbed wire if necessary

89.1

S

S

S

88.2

S

N

S

R.Wharfe

Kettleman Bridge

S

87.3

A64

A64

Avenue of trees

A659

Tadcaster

Tidewater Way

SPONSORSHIP FORM

Please send your sponsorship money to:
Tidewater Way, c/o 171 Burton
Stone Lane, York YO3 6DG. Cheques
should be made payable to 'Christian
Aid'. We will send you a receipt and
a certificate to mark your achieve-
ment if you could enclose a SAE.
Thank you for supporting Christian
Aid in this way.

Person sponsored: .... Date: ....

Name: ....

Address: ....

....

Telephone No.:..

Signature of participant:..

Signature of parent or guardian if needed): ....

Please state how the Sponsored crossing will be done –
as 24-hour challenge, team event, over several days, etc.

....

Christian Aid
Registered Charity number 258003

SPONSORS
Please enter your name and address and amount promised in the first three columns below.
When the Way has been completed, the sponsored person will return to collect the money from you.
Please enter then the total amount you pay in column 4.   *Or fixed sum

1. Name	2. Address	3. Amount promised per .... completed*	4. Total amount paid
1.			
2.			
3.			
4.			
5.			
6.			
7.			
8.			
9.			
10.			
11.			
12.			

SPONSORS

Please enter your name and address and amount promised in the first three columns below. When the Way has been completed, the sponsored person will return to collect the money from you. Please enter then the total amount you pay in column 4.

*Or fixed sum

1. Name	2. Address	3. Amount promised per .... completed*	4. Total amount paid
13.			
14.			
15.			
16.			
17.			
18.			
19.			
20.			
21.			
22.			
23.			
24.			
25.			
26.			
27.			
28.			
29.			
30.			
31.			
32.			
33.			
34.			
36.			
37.			
38.			

Signature of organiser/steward on completion (if any): ....

Tidewater Way completed in a time of: ....